CW00684717

CAN WE
GOD?

Maurice Roberts

THE BANNER OF TRUTH TRUST

THE BANNER OF TRUTH TRUST
3 Murrayfield Road, Edinburgh EH12 6EL, UK
PO Box 621, Carlisle, PA 17013, USA

*

© Maurice Roberts 2006

ISBN-10: 0 85151 933 4
ISBN-13: 978 0 85151 933 3

*

Typeset in 11/13 pt Adobe Garamond
at the Banner of Truth Trust
Printed in the USA by
VersaPress, Inc.,
East Peoria, IL.

CAN WE KNOW GOD?

This world is divided into two groups – those who know God and those who do not. There are many other differences between people, but this difference is the greatest. To be ignorant of God will have a profound influence on the way we think, work, and live our entire life. More still, on the way we die and what will happen to us after death.

It is possible to change our minds about God. Millions of people have done so. They began life with little or no interest in anything religious, but then they altered their opinion. They began, as most people begin, with the confident attitude that religion and God is 'not for them'. But then they found themselves somehow unable to shake off the inner feeling that God exists and was speaking to their heart and conscience.

It is possible to know God personally and to enjoy a life-changing experience through which we come to understand that unbelief and atheism are a mistake. We do not like having to admit that we were once wrong and misguided. But this is what always happens to those who find God and come to believe in him. They feel sorry that they began life as unbelievers. They could wish to have their childhood and youth all over again so that they might live life in a better way.

To put it like that is to remind ourselves that many of us, especially in our teenage years, have made big mistakes and got ourselves into trouble. Others manage to scramble through these early years all right, but then they get all tangled up with troubles and miseries later in life. Though people do not realize it, the real reason why they get into these troubles is closely connected to a more basic and more serious problem – they do not know God.

We all have the thought at times that this world in which we live has somehow 'gone wrong'. Why are people not kinder to one another? Why all the terrible wars that have gone on over the centuries of human history? Why all the crime, the cruelty, the abuse, the divorces and break-ups? Why all the poverty, hunger and disease on earth? Of course it is possible to put these questions out of our mind and to bury our head in the sand. The great pity is that too many people learn nothing from this serious side of life. But we are fools if we refuse to face up to reality. What is the reason why so many things in this wonderful world have so obviously 'gone wrong'?

This is a good question with which to start: How do we explain the very obvious and clear fact that there is something deeply sad about this world? The unbeliever's answer is: 'That is just the way life is and you can't do anything about it.' But this is a shallow, defeatist attitude. It is really another way of saying, 'I don't like the question, and I intend to ignore it and go back to my more comfortable enjoyments.'

The way unbelievers dodge this question is also deeply selfish. They know the world has a thousand problems but they do not want to spoil their happiness by thinking about other people's miseries. This is not only selfish; it is also stupid. Sooner or later, every one of us is going to be confronted with a serious situation. Our health will break down, or our friends will be gone – or, most serious of all, we shall be faced with death and the grave.

Let me at this point tell you something that my own father discovered as a young man. I mention it because it has an important bearing on the subject. My father was a strong man, but in his twenties he caught tuberculosis. In hospital he was critically ill. Every week other patients around him were dying and being taken away to the mortuary. Mercifully my father survived to live a long, happy, and healthy life. But amongst all the experiences in hospital he learnt a valuable lesson – that when he was ill and in need it was people who were religious that came to visit him and others like him. He himself was not a true believer in God at that time, though he became one later in life. But he never forgot this lesson: When you are in real trouble it is usually those who know God that come to help you and show you kindness.

What my father had discovered was that it changes people when they come to know God. When you trust in God you become a different person. It could be explained like this. When anyone finds God they become a new 'edition' of their former self. It is rather like an old book that is re-published in a new edition. They become new and better than ever before.

The way in which people find God is different in every case but it always leads to the same result – they become changed, and changed for the better.

But where is a person to begin if they would like to know God? Begin by listening to what God says to us all to encourage us to come to him. God says that those who love him and that those who seek him diligently will find him. To seek God means to desire to know him. The wonderful thing is that God will reveal himself to those who truly want him. Our past unbelief or our past foolishness will not be a barrier to us if we now sincerely desire to find God and to have his favour. Why not pray to God right now and ask him to reveal himself to you?

WHAT DOES IT MEAN TO BE SAVED?

To know God is to be 'saved'. To say this is the same as saying that mankind, apart from those who have come to know God, are in need of 'salvation'. This fact reflects what we said before, that the world is made up of two sorts of people, those who know God and those who do not. We could state this in another way, by saying that mankind consists of those who are saved and those who are not.

When we talk about saved people we do not refer necessarily to people who are decent, or respectable, or 'good living', but to people who have undergone a spiritual change in their lives. This change may have come about in childhood, or in adolescence, or later on in life. Not all of those who are churchgoers or respectable have undergone this change in their lives. But all who have been saved will reflect this change in the way they live, more or less.

What then does it mean to be saved? This is the most important subject in religion. It is the most serious question that we could ask.

But before we answer this question we must face the fact that there is something in us which resents having to think of being saved. For one thing, we do not like to be told that there is something which we need and do not have. It somehow hurts our pride. We want to say at once, 'I am as good as the next man and need nothing.' Or, if that is not our reaction to the idea of salvation, we are apt to feel uncomfortable and nervous. This reaction is common and it is understandable. Salvation is a subject that provokes cheap jokes on the TV chat show or in the public house. It is all too tempting to turn away from it with the apology that 'this is not for me'. But it is foolish not to find out what this idea of salvation means.

The word salvation used in religion, means being rescued from the very great danger to which we are exposed because of the wrongs we have done in this life. Putting it simply, it is this: we must after death face punishment for everything we have done wrong from the beginning to the end of our earthly life. This is true for everyone except for those who are pardoned, or saved.

Life on earth will be followed by life in eternity. We, as human beings, are going to live in another world after we die. This is not true of animals, but it is true of men and women. Human beings possess a soul; the animals do not. When animals die they are all finished; when a human being dies he or she lives in another world. The soul leaves the body and enters into eternity. The wrong things we do now in this life, if they are not pardoned, will be eternally a source of suffering and misery to us in the life to come.

Hence, we need – all of us – to seek to be saved from the consequences of our wrongdoing. This is what we mean by being saved. It is, as we said a little earlier, a most serious matter. Only a fool would joke about such a subject.

Perhaps you are ready to say, 'I never heard this teaching before.' Sadly, there are many, even church-going people, who have not had this subject of salvation made clear to them. Of course, it makes all the difference when we look at life in the light of our need to be saved. If we are all snuffed out, or wiped out, at death, then we might as well live all for pleasure and happiness now. But if we realize there is a life after this present life, in which we are going to face punishment for all our evil deeds and words, then we begin to look at life in a completely different way.

To see our need of being saved is a first step to getting this salvation. The most urgent need we all have before we are saved is to come to know the danger we are in. Jesus Christ put this point in an illustration. He said that no one goes to the doctor if he thinks he is healthy and fit. It is when we see and know that we are ill that we think of going to see a doctor. This is true of bodily illness. It is true of a person when they come to see their need of being saved.

To know our need of being saved is a tremendous help. It alters our way of thinking at once. Those who do not see their need of salvation live for this life. This explains why the society we live in is as it is. The great emphasis is all on getting money and buying more and more things. It is the search for happiness. But what good will it all do us in the end? Even supposing we owned the whole world, it would not be of any good to us in the end because we must all die and go into eternity.

On the other hand, the troubles of life and its difficult experiences will all soon be over and, if we have salvation we shall soon be in that better and blessed world called heaven. To see this is to see that nothing in this life really matters apart from getting the gift of salvation. The Bible calls salvation, therefore, 'the one thing needful'. It is the one and only thing that matters in the end.

The thought might come into our mind at this point, 'Why do not more people take an interest in this subject of being saved?' The answer is, I am afraid, a sad one. It is because so many people would rather have a 'good time' now. They are prepared to risk the future because it seems far away. But this is foolish and reckless. A wise man or woman will say, 'I would rather be saved and go to heaven than enjoy life's pleasures, and lose my own soul in the end.'

When we begin to talk like that we have taken our first step towards being saved.

HOW 'GOOD' MUST WE BE?

To get to heaven we must, of course, be 'good'. It is obvious to everyone that heaven is for good people. This faces us with the question: How good must we be to get to heaven? There have been all sorts of answers to this. But the true answer is that we must have a perfect goodness because nothing less will do. By *perfect* is meant absolutely perfect. To get to heaven we need to be faultless, flawless, and spotless in the eyes of God, who is the final and great Judge of all men.

There are two possible ways in which people might obtain this spotless perfection. They must either get it by being perfect in themselves, or, alternatively, they might get it as a gift from someone else who is able to bestow this perfection on them. There is no third possibility. Our goodness must be either a thing we obtain by our own merit and effort, or we must receive it as a gift given to us by someone who has this goodness to give away as a free gift.

It is here that people almost always go wrong when they start to take an interest in religion. When we speak of goodness in this sense we ought to use another word – *righteousness*. Let us see why.

The word righteousness is the correct term to use when we refer to the standard of goodness which God our Judge requires from us. Righteousness means reaching the level of personal obedience which satisfies the Judge. If we reach this level we shall be pronounced 'righteous' and 'blessed' and we shall be welcomed into heaven forever. On the other hand, if we fall short of the required level of obedience to what God our Judge requires of us, we shall be in the end pronounced 'unrighteous' and 'cursed'. We shall, in that event, be eternally excluded from the presence of God in heaven.

Because our future destiny is ultimately concerned in this subject, we must give it our closest attention. How can we get a perfect righteousness and so ensure a happy life in heaven in the end?

In looking for the answer to this question we must be prepared for some very humbling things to be said to us. None of us was born good or righteous. On the contrary, we are all born evil. This is unwelcome information and many people, on being told this, turn away from the whole subject of religion in disgust. They have a high opinion of themselves and take it badly when it is said to them that they are wicked. But it does us good to learn the truth about ourselves as God sees it. God tells us the worst about ourselves, not in an unkind way, but out of a loving wish to do us great good, if only we will listen to what he says.

The word we use to describe men and women as we now are is the term 'sinners'. This is not to say that all are criminals of the worst kind, but that all of us fail to reach the standard of goodness set by God as our Creator and Judge. Many people are very upright, decent, and honest. Sometimes they act nobly, generously, and very affectionately. To call such people 'sinners' is not to deny the fine qualities which they have. It is to say that, in spite of all these fine qualities, they are not as good as they should be. A 'sinner' is one who comes short of reaching the standard which God requires of us all. In the judgment of God therefore, we are *all* sinners. There is none 'righteous' – or perfectly obedient.

A part of the standard set by God is that we ought, all of us, to love our fellow men with as much affection and care as we love ourselves with. A moment's thought will tell us that we have never done so. Yet we ought to have done. If we were as good – that is to say righteous – as we should be, we would all of us love our neighbour as ourselves. We would love them in the sense that we would do them all the good we could. We would never have an unkind thought of them or say an unkind word to them. But no man ever lived who kept this standard set by God. At least, no mere man has done so. We must come back to this point later.

It is a fact that not a single person who ever lived (with one exception) has perfectly kept the standard sct for mankind by a good and loving God. However nice persons whom we may meet are, they are all 'sinners' who fall short in their obedience to the command of God to love our neighbour as ourselves. For that reason alone we are proved to be sinful. But more must be said.

A further part of the standard laid down by God is that we should love God himself with all our heart and soul and mind. This means that we owe it to God to make him the most important person in our life. We are obligated to delight our minds with the thought of God, to worship him daily, to do his revealed will, to obey his every command and, in short, to seek to please him in every possible way. To love God with all our heart can mean nothing less than this. Putting it another way, to love God means to love what he loves and to hate what he hates, to be grateful for all he gives, and to be content with what he withholds from us.

It is most just and reasonable for God to set such a standard as the above. He gave us our being by creating us. He is the Judge who is entitled to set the standard. We are his creatures, and as such we are duty-bound to do all that he requires. People may not like to feel bound by God's standards and laws. But this dislike does not in the least exempt them from the obligation to be perfectly obedient. Atheists and Agnostics are just as much obligated to obey God as other people are.

It is clear from what we have said here that we have no hope at all of being good enough for God by efforts or merit of our own. We cannot by hard work earn a place in heaven. We must get righteousness as a gift from one who is able to give it to us.

ARE WE NOT ALL GOD'S CHILDREN?

The correct answer to the question above is: Yes – and No. It all depends on what you mean by the phrase 'God's children'. A wrong but rather common way of thinking about this subject may be put in these words: 'The universal Fatherhood of God and the universal brotherhood of men.' Many people assume without question that if God made us then he must be our

Father and we must be his children. But this is misleading. The point needs to be explained.

There *is* a sense in which all men are the children of God. It is so in the sense that all men are created by God. Men and women are endowed with special faculties which distinguish us from the animals. We have intelligence, will, emotions, conscience, God-consciousness, an instinct to worship, a concept of eternity, a sense of right and wrong, etc. It is obvious that the human race has been created with gifts and powers of mind and soul which place us in a higher category than the brute beasts. We explain this by saying that men and women are created in the 'image' of God. So in this sense it is not incorrect to say that we are God's children.

But in the fullest sense we become God's children only when we know God and are saved. We have no right to think of God as our heavenly Father until we have become believers in Jesus Christ. It is most important that we understand this. When Jesus Christ taught people to address God as 'our Father', he did so on the assumption that they were disciples who looked on Jesus as their Saviour.

By nature we are all haters of God, not friends or sons of God. As God looks upon us before we wear the robe of righteousness, we are displeasing to him. A number of things are true about our relationship to God before coming to faith. There is anger in God against us. He is critical of us. He warns us of coming misery if we do not repent. He sends judgments of one sort or another on us. We grieve him by our bad behaviour. We tax his patience. We abuse his goodness. We offend him and provoke him to punish us.

It is very clear then that God is not our heavenly Father so long as the relationship between him and us is so bad.

Having said this, it is still true that God is very merciful and patient with us even when we grieve and vex him by our sinful ways. God goes on, very often, showing mercy and goodness to us in our lives even when we provoke him to be displeased with us. This goodness, which God shows to us, ought to have the effect of making us repent and turn to him. The wonderful fact about God always is that he delights in mercy and is most ready to forgive. This he will do when we humble ourselves and ask for his pardon and grace.

There are two very good reasons why we should wish to become God's children through faith in Jesus Christ. For one thing, if we are not God's children then we are the devil's children. It is for this reason that Jesus Christ said to some people that they were of their 'father the devil'. We may be shocked by the thought, but a moment's reflection will show us that this must be right. If we are wicked in our life we cannot be said to be God's children but the devil's. Those who are God's children do works that reflect the character of God.

If our religion does not make us loving, kind, and good it cannot be the religion which God has revealed to us. To spread cruelty, or lies, or fear and death is the devil's work, and those who do these things have no right to call themselves God's children.

But there is another reason why we should desire to become the children of God. It is because God promises great blessings and rewards to those who are his children. He promises them his favour in this life and eternal happiness in the life to come. Who would not wish to have so blessed a prospect? What blessings does God promise to those who through faith in Christ become his sons?

To get a complete answer to this question we must study the Bible, which is a revelation of God's mind and will. The Bible is full of the most wonderful promises made by God to us when we belong to him by faith. But the short answer is, that God promises to give us sufficient grace to help us every day we live in this world. And he also promises to give us an honoured place at last in his heavenly home, which is described as being like a large house with room for all believers. Included in his promises are the best things we can imagine. These are peace and joy now in our hearts, a felt sense of his love from day to day, and, in the world to come, a glory like that of the sun, moon, and stars.

A well-known and well-loved Christian writer, John Bunyan, explains the difference between worldly happiness and heavenly happiness in *The Pilgrim's Progress*. A man in a room has his eyes only downward and a muck-rake in his hand. Over his head stands another man with a heavenly crown in his hand, offering to the first man the crown in exchange for the muck-rake. But the foolish man neither looks up nor pays any attention, but goes on raking up straw, several sticks, and the dust on the floor.

John Bunyan, in his own vivid way, here shows us the difference between what God offers to us if we become his spiritual children and what men of this world get after a lifetime of worldly ambition. This is absolutely true. To live for this present world and to spend all our energies gathering its good things is no better than scraping together a heap of dust and straw. But if we seek God and become members of his family, we shall receive a crown of glory at last that shall never fade away.

WHO CAN GIVE US A RIGHTEOUSNESS?

If we must have a perfect righteousness in order to be saved and fit for heaven who can give us such a righteousness? This is the subject to which we now turn. As sinners we cannot give ourselves a perfect righteousness. Nor can saints or angels, however good, give us acceptance with God. Whatever of goodness they have they need for themselves. They have none to spare for others. It is impossible for angels or saints to exceed what God requires of them so as to possess an 'extra', which they can give away to the rest of us. This is the heart of our problem as sinners. We do not have a perfect righteousness of our own and no other created being can give us one.

But what is impossible with men is – wonderful to say – possible with God. Here is the good news. God himself freely offers to all mankind a perfect righteousness. We are invited to go to God for it. We may ask him for it. This righteousness is like a robe that covers our nakedness and cloaks all our guilt and sin. Those who receive this robe of righteousness wear it now in this life; and they will wear it forever in heaven. This is the difference between false religion and true. False forms of religion teach people to make themselves good enough for God. True religion tells men to despair of all self-made righteousness and to seek a God-given righteousness, which he freely gives to all who ask for it.

You can verify this for yourself. However much you try to make yourself good enough for God you will find in the end it is a failure. The reason is that all our goodness is never good enough. But then, go to God and plead with him to give you the free gift of righteousness, and when you have it you will *feel* the difference.

The way we feel it is in our heart and in our conscience. It is a deep peace, a realization that we are right with God, an experience of comfort. There are very many books telling how people got this experience and what they felt when they got it. Each person expresses it in a slightly different way. But it all amounts to the same thing.

To get this gift of righteousness from God is the greatest and best experience we could ever have in all our life. Lots of people are trying out experiences of one kind or another in these days: drugs of various kinds and ways of getting a 'kick'. But not one of these things can be compared with the inward joy, peace, and assurance that come when we get right with God. To get right with God is an experience that changes us radically and forever. It is a 'heaven-on-earth' experience. It satisfies us fully. And it does us only good and – unlike drink and drugs – it does us no harm.

It is essential to understand how God has provided for mankind this gift of righteousness about which we are speaking. This gift is not something which he *created* in the same way that he created heaven and earth. Rather, it was brought into being by a wonderful series of divine actions done by a special person in the course of human history.

God the Father sent his Son Jesus Christ into the world two thousand years ago. Jesus came to save us by keeping God's law for us and then by dying on the cross for us. His life was perfect. His death was a sacrifice. In love for the world God sent Christ to do for us what we could not do for ourselves.

We cannot live a righteous life; but Jesus Christ did. We cannot satisfy God's righteous standards; but Jesus Christ did. We cannot make amends for our sins and faults; but Jesus did. In so doing, Christ worked out a perfect righteousness. And because Christ is the Son of God this righteousness is infinitely precious to God the Father.

Jesus' life and death together form one great transaction by which he makes satisfaction to God by shedding his blood, and also fulfils the righteousness of God's law as our Representative and Substitute. We shall never understand how to become righteous if we do not see who Jesus Christ is and appreciate what he has done for us.

Christ is not an ordinary person like ourselves. He is a divine person. As the Son of God he took our human nature so that he might act as a Representative and Substitute for us. He lived a perfect life as our Representative. He died a sacrificial death as our Substitute. His life and death were necessary in different ways. His perfect life was lived so that it could be 'given' to us – or, if you like, accredited to us. His sacrificial death was died to satisfy the offended justice of God. By 'offended' here we mean that God is insulted and made angry by human disobedience. But Jesus' death was died to pay for the outrage that our sins have done to God's perfect justice.

The righteousness therefore which God freely offers to us is that which Christ has obtained for us by life and death. Let us see just two or three more things at this stage:

How do I know that Christ's righteousness is enough to make me acceptable with God?

The answer is: Because God raised Christ from the dead on the third day after he died on the cross. Had Christ not been raised, we would have no hope. But God raised Christ from the dead to reassure us all that the righteousness obtained for us by Christ is fully and entirely sufficient to bring us to God.

How can I obtain this perfect righteousness? To get this wonderful blessing it is essential to put from us all thought of making ourselves worthy. God requires of us just this: faith. By faith we receive the gift of a God-given righteousness. By faith we come into a condition of being right with God and fit for heaven.

It is usual for people to feel surprise when they hear this message. To get so good a gift and to pay nothing for it seems like cheating! 'Can we not at least pay God back by giving some good works of our own?' No, we must not try to do so – and this for these good reasons. If we could 'pay' for this gift of God we would start to boast about the fact. Above all, Christ has paid the price for us – in full.

IS THERE LIFE AFTER DEATH?

It is natural for people to ask if there is a life beyond death. After all, we must die sooner or later. It is foolish to close our minds to a subject which is so obviously important. Besides, it will have an effect on the way we live now if we have clear knowledge about the after-life. On the other hand, to live in ignorance of life-after-death could mean to end up in a hopeless situation from which we could have escaped if only we had taken careful action in time.

An obvious way to explain this is to think of a house-fire. If fire breaks out while the people in the house are awake, there is a reasonable chance that they will get out in time. But if they are all fast asleep, they are in a much more perilous position. They risk being burnt to death.

This is exactly the case when it comes to the after-life. If we have correct knowledge of what we are going to meet after death we can prepare for it. But if we have no idea what lies ahead of us in a state of death we can hardly expect to be ready to face it. The illustration is perfectly correct. This is an essential and most vital subject for us all to know about.

For all men and women who are worthy, life after death will be a happy thing. The change which we refer to as 'death' means that the soul leaves the body and enters into 'paradise' or 'heaven'. The body is then placed in a coffin and is buried in the earth. At funeral services, when this happens, it is common for people to say 'dust to dust, ashes to ashes' – or some such expression. This is a reminder to us that our human body was at first made from the dust of the ground by God. So at death the 'dust', which was our earthly body in this life, returns to the 'dust' into which it is now to be buried.

Much more important than what happens to our body at death is what then happens to the soul. In the case of those who die as believers, their soul immediately appears in the presence of God and of Jesus Christ in paradise. In this life the soul lives within the body, but after death the soul is 'naked' or 'disembodied'. It enters, without the body, into a state of peace and rest after the storms of life. The blessed dead, as we may call them, are now perfectly holy. All their weaknesses and sins are forever over and past. Their condition is that of moral perfection and sinlessness. They are conscious in death and they enjoy the happy company of God, of Christ, of the angels, and of all other saints who have died as they now have.

However, though the blessed dead are perfectly holy and at peace, they have not yet arrived at the state of final completeness. They do not yet have their body. So the blessed dead look forward to the end of the world when their bodies will be restored to them.

This event will occur at a time known only to God. When that solemn hour arrives, the great trumpet will be blown and all the dead will rise out of the earth and out of the sea – depending on where death has occurred. The body of every saint will then be rejoined by the soul. In a body, which is now shining like the sun, each resurrected believer will rise up to meet Jesus Christ in the clouds as he now comes to judge all people who have ever lived.

At this judgment the righteous will be honoured by Christ and then brought by him into the renewed universe, which is described as the 'new heavens and new earth'. This is the final and eternal home of the faithful. God will be their all in all for evermore. Their happiness will be ecstatic, their satisfaction complete, and their joys sublime to all eternity. They will be rewarded by Christ for all the service which they rendered to him in this world. This reward will more than make up for all their tears and sorrows in this present life. All their troubles now are over.

We may think of heaven, then, as coming to God's believing people in two stages: at death, and after the resurrection. We refer to the state of the blessed dead in the period between death and the resurrection as the Intermediate State. The state of believers after the resurrection and judgment is referred to as the Final State.

But what of those who are unbelievers? This question brings us face to face with the most solemn subject in religion. After death the soul of the unbeliever enters into the Intermediate State of hell and remains there in pain, misery, and punishment till the end of the world. The body of each unbeliever will then be resurrected at the same time as the righteous are raised. But the bodies of the wicked will be repulsive in appearance.

After the judgment they will be sent forever into the Final State of hell. Here they will be punished forever with the most terrible pains of soul and body. Jesus Christ speaks of this place of hell very often in his teaching so as to warn us. He urges us to prepare for death by repenting of all our sins and by believing in him as our Saviour and Lord.

Hell is a place and a state of misery from which no one can escape. God created it like a prison. Here those who have dishonoured God by their way of life on earth must suffer for the wrongs they have done. The reason why hell never ends is because sin is an infinite evil and cannot be pardoned except when in this life we repent and believe in Jesus Christ. A famous poet called Dante once wrote that over the entrance to hell are the words, 'Abandon hope all who enter here.' Though Dante was not an inspired writer, this is a correct thought and a deeply solemn truth. Those who enter hell have no hope because their punishment will never, never end.

This is why God lovingly invites us all to believe in Christ NOW, before it is too late.

HOW CAN WE BE SURE WHAT TO BELIEVE ?

A common and understandable problem which many have when they think of religious subjects is this: How can we know what is correct and what is false? In matters of science we can weigh and measure with our own eyes. But how do we do this in religion?

One man's creed seems to be another man's heresy. If it is all guesswork, we may be believing only in the empty ghosts of men's minds. If there is no objective standard by which to measure religious ideas then we can never be sure of anything in matters of faith. What we most need then is a sure rule from which to draw our creed and frame our conduct.

The rule of faith is not man's mind. Nor is it some religious tradition handed down by one or other of the world's religions: God has not left us in the uncertain position of having no clear source of knowledge in matters of faith and worship.

The place from which we must get all our knowledge of God is the Bible, which consists of the Old and New Testaments. The Old Testament was written in Hebrew (with a few parts in Aramaic) before the coming of Christ two thousand years ago. The New Testament was written in Greek shortly after the life and ministry of Christ was completed.

Christians say that the Bible is 'the Word of God'. It is inspired revelation. It is comparable to a light shining in a dark place to show us the way. It functions as a lamp to light up the path of life. It is the measuring line by which we are to judge all religious opinions and traditions. If the things we believe are fully consistent with the teaching of the Bible then we are 'sound in the faith'. If not, we are in error. Jesus Christ, the Son of God, always pointed people to the Bible. The phrase 'It is written' was used by Jesus to settle any point of doctrine, or conclude any dispute about what to believe and how to worship God. We are to do the same.

It is possible to go far wrong in religion by not keeping strictly to this method of testing and proving what we hear in matters of religious faith and practice. Christ expresses this point in a memorable way. He says that if the light in us is darkness, how great is that darkness! He means that if we have a creed and a religion which are false, we are in a fearfully deluded state. This of course is the case with many people. They believe fervently in things that have not come from the Bible, and so they are in a pitiable condition.

Since Jesus Christ is the Son of God, who was sent into the world to teach us how to know God, we ought to take the same view of the Holy Bible that he took of it. Jesus' attitude to the Bible is easy to find out. It is found in the four Gospels at the beginning of the New Testament. In praying to God his Father he says that God's Word, the Bible, is 'truth'. He says, 'Scripture cannot be broken.' He even states that heaven and earth will pass away, but his words will not pass away.

This is the view which Christ had of the Bible, and it was one that was consistent and unvarying. He spoke out strongly against some religious leaders in his day who added ideas of men to the Bible. He taught us to respect the Bible as uniquely God's revelation to mankind. He told those who added their own human traditions to God's Word that they were guilty of taking away 'the key of knowledge'. By that he meant the pure unadulterated teaching which God gives us in the Bible, as compared with the unscriptural teachings that men had invented out of their own brains.

This view of the Bible, which Christ taught, is the view of it which his apostles taught also. Peter and Paul, James and John, as well as all the other New Testament writers, had this same attitude to the Bible. This was the rule by which Christ and the apostles taught us to test and to prove all religious teachings and practices.

There is no need to complicate our quest as we seek to know God. The Bible is the light we need. It is sufficient to bring us to God. It is the revelation of God's mind and will to the whole world. Thousands of men and women over the centuries of past history have lived and died with the hope of heaven in their hearts because they made God's Word their daily study.

✳ BANK OF SCOTLAND

4543 1313 1584 9525

04/06   04/09 ✓

MR A N MCLACHLAN
07 01 16 06719911   0657

BANNER OF TRUTH TS
EDINBURGH   BOS

	DATE	SEND?	TAKE?
	25/4/07		
	SALES No.	INITIALS	
DEPT.			
QUANTITY AND DESCRIPTION			
Books			
MERCHANT USE ONLY			
PURCHASING CARD USE ONLY			
TOTAL £		8=40	

PLEASE KEEP THIS COPY FOR YOUR RECORDS

SALE CONFIRMED - CARDHOLDER'S SIGNATURE	AUTHORISATION CODE
	101

CARDHOLDER'S DECLARATION: The issuer of the card identified on this item is authorised to pay the amount shown as TOTAL upon proper presentation. I promise to pay such TOTAL (together with any other charges due thereon) subject to and in accordance with the agreement governing the use of such card.

Thousands of men and women all over the world today, on all continents and in many different languages, have found God for themselves as they have read the Bible and heard its message preached to them.

Jesus Christ uses a notable illustration in his famous Sermon on the Mount to describe what we are to think of those who live their life by the Bible, and those who do not. Those who believe God's Word, and live according to its teaching, are to be compared to a man who builds his house on a rock. When the rains fall, the winds blow hard, and the floods rise up, the house is secure because it is founded on a rock. On the other hand, those who believe things that the Bible does not teach, and live their lives in some way that is not according to God's Word, are like a man who builds his house on the sand. When the storm comes the house will collapse.

This illustration is a reminder to us that this discussion about the Bible is not a merely theoretical one. It is intensely practical. The way we believe and live is soon going to be tested by God himself in the course of this life – and ultimately on the great Day of Judgment. If we are sound in our faith and are living in the light of God's Word we shall be safe at last. When God searches out our entire life's work on the Last Day, he will commend us and reward us eternally if we have built our life on what he tells us in the Bible. But if we go by human speculations and man-made ideas, however popular they may be for a time, we shall meet disaster in that great Day.

Could any subject be more serious?

CAN WE BE SURE WE ARE SAVED?

The message of Jesus Christ is called the 'gospel'. The word means 'good news'. The good news is that God freely offers eternal life to all who repent and believe in Christ as their Saviour. This good news is not offered to any special class of people. It is offered to all in every nation who hear it. The only condition of salvation is that we believe. When we believe in Christ we at once have this promised life from God. We do not need to wait till the hour of death to get it. The way the apostle John puts it is simple and clear: 'Whoever has the Son has life; whoever does not have the Son of God does not have life' (*1 John* 5:12). So the instant we put our trust in God's Son for salvation we are saved.

Once we are saved we are saved forever. It is not possible for a true believer to be lost. God's promise is that when we believe his gospel we are at once pardoned all our sins and are all our life kept by his power till at death we enter into paradise. We refer to this part of the gospel's wonderful teaching as 'perseverance'.

The apostle Peter says that by God's power all believers are being guarded through faith till they come to salvation (*1 Peter* 1:5). The apostle Paul declares wonderfully that nothing 'will be able to separate us from the love of God' (*Romans* 8:39). Christ himself expresses this same sweet truth when he says that no one is able to snatch believers out of the heavenly Father's hand (*John* 10:29).

So God does not offer us a doubtful salvation. He saves the believer and also keeps him in a state of salvation all through life. It would be terrible to have a kind of salvation that could be had one day and lost the next. Even the sins and faults of a believer, bad as they are, cannot put the believer back again into his previous lost state. If they did, we could never be sure that we are saved. We would always be in doubt and fear. And this fear would be torment.

In his kindness and love God gives to believers an assurance that they are saved. We may refer to this assurance as the 'cream' of salvation in this life. It is the happy and comforting certainty that we belong to God as children to a Father. It is the cheering and exciting realization that we are now God's sons and daughters on the path that leads to heaven. This certainty which believers have lifts us above outward trials and miseries and helps us to look beyond the things that upset us in this life. If we know we are soon to be with God in glory why should we be overmuch troubled by life's little worries or cares?

God is so extremely kind to believers that he gives them more than one means of being assured of their salvation. This is something that is always true about God in the gospel. It is his abundant kindness and his overflowing generosity to those who believe and receive what he promises to us in the Bible. We can put it like this. God always does what is 'God-like'. He always behaves in a way that reflects his own good and gracious character. God will never act in a way that is unworthy of himself. On the contrary, he is 'rich in mercy'. God is wonderfully full of love and faithfulness. These are expressions used in the Bible to tell us about God's character.

There are at least three ways in which God assures his people that they are saved. These are: by the Bible, by the noticeable change in our own life, and by his Holy Spirit in our heart. Let us consider these points.

The Bible contains many heart-warming statements which inform us as believers that we have every right to think we are saved. Jesus Christ says this: 'I am the bread of life.' Those who come to him shall not hunger (*John* 6:35). Again, Jesus says to us all: 'I am the light of the world.' Those who follow him will not walk in darkness (*John* 8:12). Again, Christ says that his sheep hear his voice. He knows them, and they follow him. He gives them eternal life, and they will never perish (*John* 10:27–28). The obvious meaning of these and all such words is that to have Christ as our Lord and Saviour is to have food for our soul, light for our path in life, and eternal salvation at last.

There is a second way by which God assures the believer that he is saved and therefore safe. It is by the change that has come about in our own life. When we become God's children by faith in Christ we are conscious that we are not the people we were before. The believer is now holy in his character. This is not to say he is perfect but his heart now has a genuine love for God and for fellowship with like-minded believers. This is not true of others.

The world does not love God, nor does it love God's people. It cannot understand or appreciate them. But if we see in ourselves a sincere love for Christ, for the Bible, for the company of other believers, for prayer, and for more obedience to God's will – then we are to conclude that we are saved. We may take these inward desires for God as signs that we have come to know him. It is sadly true that some people show some of these signs for a time, but then drift back into the world. Such people are not God's children. God's children continue in these things to the end of their lives.

The third way by which God gives assurance to his children is by an inward influence of his Holy Spirit. The Holy Spirit is a Person of the Godhead. His ministry is to be our Comforter in this present life and to prepare us as God's children for our heavenly home. The Spirit lives in the soul of a believer. He pours into our soul a sense of God's love for us in the here and now of this life. We know how comforting it is to have a sense of being loved and cared for by another human person. Much more comforting is this inward experience of warmth, love, and peace, which the Spirit of God puts in our heart.

This inward influence of God's Spirit in the heart is sometimes called a 'seal' or a 'witness'. Its effect is to make us sure that we know God. It is wonderful to know God. But it is more wonderful still to *know* that we know him. It is a real 'heaven upon earth'. It not only makes the believer strong but it makes him joyful and thankful. It also tends to make him more holy because it stirs him up to watch and pray, to seek after God, and to do his will.

WHAT DO CHRIST AND THE APOSTLES TEACH ABOUT HELL?

The difference between a real believer in the gospel and a false one is this: one accepts *all* that God's Word teaches, while the other believes only what suits him. There are in the teachings of the Bible both sweet and bitter things – things to make us glad and things to make us sad. We have no right to believe only what is sweet and comforting. We must take all that God says because it comes to us with his divine authority. To discard the parts of God's Word which we may not like is to make God a liar. It is also a sign that we are not God's children. God's children meekly accept whatever they find written in Holy Scripture.

No one who reads the New Testament could possibly doubt that Christ and his apostles teach us that there is a place called hell. There is a reference to it in almost every book of the New Testament. For instance, Christ tells us in the Sermon on the Mount about people with unfruitful lives who are thrown into the fire (*Matthew* 7:19). He warns us not to fear men but only God who 'can destroy both soul and body in hell' (*Matthew* 10:28). Christ tells us that it is better to cut off everything that hinders us from getting to heaven rather than to be thrown into hell. Hell is a place where their 'worm does not die' and the 'fire is not quenched' (*Mark* 9:43, 47-48). He describes the condition of a certain lost sinner. This unhappy man was rich while he was on earth but now he is in torment in hell (*Luke* 16:23). These and many similar passages prove that Christ teaches there really is a place called hell.

It is understandable that people do not like to be told about hell. The very word has a doleful sound to it. The thought is to us fearful that God will one day cast some people, body and soul, into a great fire forever. It seems at first sight to be both dreadful and offensive even to speak about hell. But if such a place exists, as Christ and the apostles tell us, then we would be fools to turn a blind eye to this teaching. Indeed, there are good reasons why we should be very grateful to be told about hell.

For one thing, we need to see that God tells us about hell to warn us against ending up there. If a tidal wave is on the way to our lovely warm seaside while we are sunbathing on the shore, we would be completely foolish not to be grateful for a warning. If we know that the aeroplane we are waiting to board is sure to crash we would not get on it to start with. So it is with hell. If it is coming to people who have no faith in God, or in the gospel, it is only a kindness to warn them. The hope is that in this way people will start to seek God and begin to pay attention to the gospel of Christ. So, it is really a mark of God's goodness and kindness that he tells us about hell in good time. Wise people will take the necessary steps to be prepared so that they never go there.

Then too, the Bible's teaching about hell is good for us all now, and it is good for society as a whole. Sin is not just a word – it is a reality. Murder, adultery, torture, oppression, and theft are all real problems in the real world. They are so pressing and urgent that governments and police can sometimes scarcely control them. Crime is a way of life for many thousands of people who care nothing for the misery they inflict on others if only they can get what they want.

So people everywhere need to be told about hell. The doctrine of eternal punishment, even when it may not make people turn to God, may have the effect of deterring people from crime. If they know there is to be a punishment after death for our crimes in this life, many people will keep away from crime to avoid – as they hope – the prospect of being cast into hell fire.

But the main reason why God's Word tells us about hell is to bring us to repentance and faith. This is why so many great preachers, like Christ and his apostles, have, over the course of the years, preached about hell to their congregations. Another case is that of John the Baptist who spoke very strong words to his hearers. He addressed them as a 'brood of vipers'! He warned them to flee from the wrath to come (*Luke* 3:7). Sin is not a small or light thing. Sinners are, in God's sight, like poisonous snakes. They injure and kill others, as some serpents can do.

The message of warning is also not a casual or half-hearted thing. It is a trumpet-call to wake people up to see what they will have to suffer if they are not brought to repentance. So, they must be told honestly and earnestly to 'flee from the wrath to come'.

This wrath is nothing less than the just judgment of God on our sinful lives. It is the same thing as having to go to prison forever in another world. It is to be beaten by God for our wicked unbelief and disobedience to his commands. It is to be cast into a lake of fire, and there to be left. It is to go into outer darkness, far from God and far from all our present comforts and pleasures. It is to be forever in the company of Satan and all the other devils. Could anything be more dreadful or more terrifying?

We would despair if we were told of hell and not also told how to escape from it. God in his grace and mercy has explained in his Word how we may escape. The gospel of Christ is the message which tells us how we may 'flee from the wrath to come' and escape from the terrible effects of sin in our own hearts, and the terrible punishment which sinners face.

The message of the gospel is this: Jesus Christ, the eternal Son of God, came into this world two thousand years ago to die in our place. On the cross Jesus underwent unspeakable pains and sufferings. This he did for our sakes. In his great love for poor sinners, God laid on Jesus Christ the punishments and torments that we deserve. In this way God's justice has been perfectly satisfied. Even though we sinners do not deserve it, we may have all the glories of heaven after we die. This we certainly and undoubtedly will enjoy if in this life we repent of sin and put our trust in Christ as our Saviour.

The Bible states that whoever believes in the Son of God has eternal life. On the other hand whoever does not obey the Son shall not see life, but the wrath of God remains on him. You can read these words in John's Gospel, chapter 3, and at verse 36. John's Gospel is a very good place to start reading the Bible.

WHAT DO CHRIST AND THE APOSTLES TEACH ABOUT HEAVEN?

God made us for himself and we can only be fully happy when we find our happiness in him. When we read the Bible we see that it was God's purpose, not to give believers their highest happiness in this world, but to give it to us in the world to come. That world is heaven. Christ and his apostles speak very often about this blessed world above.

We have to prepare ourselves for criticism and even scoffing when we talk about heaven. For some reason worldly people take pleasure in being sarcastic when they hear us talking about the subject of heaven. The same is true when we begin to speak about anything to do with God. To the believer this scoffing and sarcastic attitude is a further proof that the Bible is correct when it tells us that the heart of man is corrupt. If it were not corrupt, people would, as they should, be delighted to talk about the happy world of heaven where all the righteous are to be together with God at last.

Since heaven is a place and a state far above all our thought or imagination, God pictures it for us in his Word by giving us various illustrations. Each one of these conveys one aspect or another of the wonderful nature of this heavenly world, which will be the 'everlasting rest' of all who love God. So, we read that it is to be a city, a kingdom, a house with many rooms, a 'new heavens and new earth'. In this celestial place all the inhabitants will be safe from all hurt, free from all fear, satisfied in all their needs, filled with every kind of blessedness and comforted after all their sufferings in this present world. They will not need to be busied with such cares as we have in this present life about money, jobs or daily food. God will in a wondrous way give to them all that they need.

So close to God will they be that they will see his face and be able to speak to him. They will know, love and be loved by those three blessed Persons of the Godhead: the Father, the Son, and the Holy Spirit. The saints in glory will shine like the sun. Their resurrection bodies will be perfectly suited to their heavenly surroundings.

Each believer will love all others and be loved by them. Heaven is a world of light, of joy, and of love. Holiness will be the hallmark of every being who is there – redeemed men and women, angels, and, above all, the great God himself. All will worship and praise this excellent, loving, and holy God. And all will have a deep sense of thankfulness to God for his unspeakable goodness to them.

In heaven some saints will have more honour than others because in this life they served God more faithfully. This will be their reward. But no such thing as jealousy will creep into the mind of any in heaven. Those who have least honour will rejoice at those who have most. Those who have much honour will show the utmost kindness to those who have less. All will be fully content with their measure and degree of honour which God has seen fit to give them. Though there will be different degrees of glory, all the people of God will be overwhelmingly happy and will be filled to the highest capacity with joy and gladness.

So God will be all in all to all his people in their final state of glory. They will discover that whatever kindness they did in this life for Jesus Christ and his people they will be abundantly rewarded in the world to come. Even if the kindness amounted to no more than giving a cup of cold water, it will be repaid to them by Christ himself at last.

In this final and heavenly state believers will know God in a far richer and fuller way than they do on earth. Their present understanding of God and of his ways is like that of children when they are young. But our understanding of God in glory will be vastly higher and greater.

There we shall see that God did everything in human history and in our own lives with perfect wisdom. There we shall see that even the trials and evils of our earthly life were all made to do us good. God's ways with us and others in life and death will then be seen in their true light. In the end believers will see that God has done all things well.

To all this happiness – and vastly more which we cannot now know or tell – will be added this: that the happiness of heaven will be *forever.* A time will never come when this blessedness will end.

Who but a fool would wish to miss the happiness of heaven? It begins here on earth, once we have come to know God, as he is revealed in Christ.

For details of other helpful publications and
free illustrated catalogue please write to

THE BANNER OF TRUTH TRUST

3 Murrayfield Road,   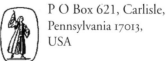   P O Box 621, Carlisle,
Edinburgh EH12 6EL   Pennsylvania 17013,
UK   USA

www.banneroftruth.co.uk